HIPSTER PUPPIES

HIPST

ER
PUPPIES

CHRISTOPHER R. WEINGARTEN

NEW AMERICAN LIBRARY

New American Library
Published by New American Library, a division of
Penguin Group (USA) Inc., 375 Hudson Street,
New York, New York 10014, USA
Penguin Group (Canada), 90 Eglinton Avenue East, Suite 700, Toronto,
Ontario M4P 2Y3, Canada (a division of Pearson Penguin Canada Inc.)
Penguin Books Ltd., 80 Strand, London WC2R 0RL, England
Penguin Ireland, 25 St. Stephen's Green, Dublin 2,
Ireland (a division of Penguin Books Ltd.)
Penguin Group (Australia), 250 Camberwell Road, Camberwell, Victoria 3124,
Australia (a division of Pearson Australia Group Pty. Ltd.)
Penguin Books India Pvt. Ltd., 11 Community Centre, Panchsheel Park,
New Delhi - 110 017, India
Penguin Group (NZ), 67 Apollo Drive, Rosedale, Auckland 0632,
New Zealand (a division of Pearson New Zealand Ltd.)
Penguin Books (South Africa) (Pty.) Ltd., 24 Sturdee Avenue,
Rosebank, Johannesburg 2196, South Africa

Penguin Books Ltd., Registered Offices:
80 Strand, London WC2R 0RL, England

First published by New American Library,
a division of Penguin Group (USA) Inc.

First Printing, July 2011
10 9 8 7 6 5 4 3 2 1

 REGISTERED TRADEMARK—MARCA REGISTRADA

Set in Bethold Akidenz Grotesk
Designed by Pauline Neuwirth

Printed in China

FOR MOM

A SPECIAL MESSAGE TO THE PEOPLE OF THE FUTURE!

Greetings from 2010 to the distant future's archeologists, the excavators of half-realized time capsules and our potential alien overlords. . . . Congratulations! You have truly made a wonderful discovery on this day!

Welcome to *Hipster Puppies*, the inaugural recipient of the Pulitzer Prize for Snarky Animal-Based Captions, Toilet-Tank Division. I'd like to thank you in advance for actually reading the humble introduction to this tome. Traditionally, the people of my era use this time to rapidly flip through the pages and mutter indignantly about how they could have just as easily written this shit.

I'd like to tell you a little about my life in 2010. I live in a borough called "Brooklyn." It was originally settled by the Dutch, which is why its inhabitants are colloquially called variations on the archaic term "*dutchbag.*" In 2010, Brooklyn's poorest and most listless citizens rule. This is because we have long since abandoned paper money in favor of a makeshift economy made solely of cocaine, toothy blow jobs and "cred." Our national language is smugness. A city council meeting unanimously agreed that our motto should just be a pair of rolled eyes, which we lovingly stitched to a flag made of American Apparel hoodies, party flyers and beard lice. Our state flower is fuck this shit.

If our citizens have one thing in common, it's that we all loathe being called "hipsters."

Currently, lexicologists have confirmed approximately 48,000 different meanings for the word "hipster." The one most agree on is "anyone who cares more about music and fashion than me." In Brooklyn, we say "hipster" about 300 times a day, upending words like "would" and "which" in the list of most commonly used words in the Brooklyn-English vernacular.

In other parts of our country, making fun of hipsters is a national pastime. I would gladly tell you about the "rest of America," had I ever a reason to leave Brooklyn for any reason whatsoever. According to the folk tales passed down from the leader of my food co-op, the "rest of America" has things like Burger Kings, non-free-trade coffee, fat people and sincerity—all of which sound completely terrifying! I have heard foul rumors that citizens in "outer-Brooklyn" often go entire weeks without eating a falafel—and many would actually pay less than $40 for a haircut. My frail bones would quake at the very thought were they not nearly dissolved from years of recreationally abusing psychotropic drugs.

To capitalize on Brooklyn's self-loathing and the rest of America's irrational hatred of us, there's a booming industry of cultural studies textbooks about the "hipster

phenomenon." Books like *Look at This Fucking Hipster,*
The Hipster Handbook and *Stuff Hipsters Hate* are dry and
completely humorless accounts of our humble civilization.

The book you hold in your hands is different since it has
the "added value" of including cute pictures of dogs.
(Dogs were animals we had domesticated and kept as
companions before the recession forced us to use them
as food.) Writing this book has been an unending joy.
Entire days of my life were spent looking at pictures of
adorable pups until I broke my "awwww" bone.

So read this book with an open mind, an open heart and
an open wallet. And please remember that hipster puppies
are people too.

Now, if you'll excuse me, this unemployment check isn't
going to cash itself.

Farewell and who gives a shit,

> Christopher R. Weingarten
> Associate Professor of the
> James Murphy Memorial Institute
> for Hipster Studies
> Brooklyn, New York

HIPSTER PUPPIES

hanzo is a graduate of the school of life…and a dropout of the pratt institute school of art and design

sasha says she's "freegan" but honestly just likes eating from the trash

sure, paddington will tell you why wes anderson is a total hack, got an hour?

barney is more concerned with "dynamic range compression"
and "the loudness wars" than the fact that he has shitty taste
in music

frequently used words that pippin's iphone autorecognizes:
douchenozzle, douchery, artfuck, jagoff, assholery

mandy considers herself a "francophile" because she owns two daft punk records

these are jules's "dress chucks"

annie is the "mom" of her squat since she does dishes and
owns dishes

camilla has to pee in the bathtub because she turned her toilet tank into a bong

bagel spent $18 on nitrate-free bacon and $16 on his wife's anniversary gift

maeby was just sober enough to translate her tattoo idea into french

quincy thinks this unagi is too salty, and he knows because
he lived in japan for a month

hank owns nine guitar pedals and knows six guitar chords

jack is a strict vegan except for fish, some chicken, honey, gummi worms, yogurt and white castle hamburgers

mattie was already caught mispronouncing "bourgeoisie" and isn't going to make the same mistake with "gauche"

bubbles wonders if obama's health care plan covers tattoo removal

don't use the term "world music" around thurston unless you want a 20-minute lecture

fearrington is running late to critical mass—could you give him a ride in your van?

popsicle wore sunglasses to a wedding

layla wants to cancel band practice this week because
30 rock is on

tilly only smokes american spirits but will drink practically anything

of course i'm the dj; i brought an ipod, didn't i?

stella's friday wardrobe includes nonprescription eyeglasses
worn over prescription contact lenses

ezra would have zero functional bathroom furniture were it not for a moist stack of old *vice* magazines

boxcar laughs at you for paying bus fare, even though it
takes her twice as long to skate to the whole foods

fuck you, asshole urban outfitters manager, i only wore it like
four times

lola got booted from the food co-op after just showing up
every week and drinking

olive hasn't exactly grasped the difference between "vintage" and "old and shitty"

after last night, eleanor better get checked for fleas and hpv

mgmt better go on soon because milo just sweated off his
nicorette patch

scottie's itunes folder is better organized than his life

emma rearranged the staff picks at the video store to reflect her sudden, irrational hate of gus fucking van sant

caina keeps his weed in a pringles can and his pringles
under his bed

ivory is a little bit rebecca, a little bit enid and completely
unbearable

using apricot shampoo only makes chewy's neckbeard
moderately less revolting

indy describes every wine as "oaky"

in the course of any given month, baby rides her skateboard once and pushes her laundry bag on it twice

popeye insists he doesn't have "a thing for asian girls," even though his last four girlfriends have been pekingese

being neutered means saving $12 a month on a suicide girls account

nat will know he lost enough weight when he goes from "girl jeans" to "child husky jeans"

"i'm a radical, not a liberal," said jasper through a mouthful of mcdonald's french fries

magoo is going to ask his fiancée if they can walk down the aisle to hüsker dü

andy knows there's no sign on the bike rack with his name
on it, but come on, man

margi tells people she does "graphic design" for a living, but in reality does "nothing"

buster will take you to a burrito place where there's "real mexicans"

dear nikon, how do you get red stripe and puke out of a d3000 digital slr camera? signed, mr. muffins

oliver flunked out of art school, but it's too bad his professors couldn't see how well he could paint snagglepuss onto a bong

peanut waited all night for his kanye air yeezys, but lost his temper within 15 minutes of the arby's drive-thru

perry could have easily informed the waiter that his order was wrong, but has decided to just write a bad yelp review instead

max refuses to eat at that restaurant because he doesn't like their font

noodles would never take a job where he had to cover up his
tattoos, were he hypothetically employable

no one responded to leopold's roommate wanted ad because he used the word "chillaxed" twice

poncho ebays old sega games and writes them off on his taxes since he "technically works with computers"

rita needs to know the "bathroom sitch" at the club tonight, because she's on day five of the master cleanse

every day is saturday when you have a trust fund

corky is sad he left his cat at the animal shelter, but mostly embarrassed they found out he named it "wikipedia morrissey IV"

hec-lin totes has hella tapeworms, y'all

isabelle's new punk band is called bed, bath and beyoncé

sophie says she's "1/8th cherokee" but really means "took a sociology class"

dodger says the words "bike culture" out loud at least once a day

ivan weeped at the sigur rós show but didn't cry at his dad's
funeral

funemployment math: one cup of coffee = ability to hang in coffee shop for two and a half hours

flower arrogantly insists that she "doesn't even own a tv," but still watches *mad men* and *arrested development* on her macbook pro

lucy and lio are living proof there is love after hooking up in a bonnaroo port-a-john

i've had all my shots . . . can i buy you one?

lucie got a band tattoo covered up by another band tattoo

remy knows heineken is exponentially better than pbr, but
he's not spending an extra dollar

winston takes better care of his records than his pet lizard

yuppies are ruining the neighborhood that snuffy already
ruined

xabe considers fixed gear bicycles to be "zenlike" and
organized religion to be "stupid"

ace requested that his new black metal band's logo be drawn "incomprehensible" but not "indecipherable"

rocko has the most enviable collection of unread chuck
klosterman books on the whole dorm floor

in the span of one day, buckley broke up with one girl over text message and hooked up with another girl over text message

tanner used his ipad to squish a bug

ernie earnestly googles for fake nudes of laurie anderson

lucia regularly drinks kombucha but couldn't tell you what it is or what it does

betsey will have her vodka without red bull because she gave up caffeine for lent

at some point, rufio got "irony" confused with "being a total fucking asshole"

beans could totally be the next dave eggers if he just lived in san francisco, had an interesting background and knew how to write

one day mischa will tell her grandkids the story of how she served coffee to interpol

lucky will gladly spend $800 on stereo equipment, but he'll
be damned if he'll pay for a prostate exam

arlo says the bullshit "no taping" policy at bb king's blues club is a "third reich thought police tactic" and that it's a tragedy this ween show will go undocumented

today, gus cleaned his sneakers with a toothbrush and cleaned his teeth with his paw

no, gary, I will not give you a ride to the fucking farmer's market

stan spent $8.95 on organic, no-salt peanut butter and then just ate his own poop

hells fucking yeah, sioux city needs another new wave band

geppetto ranked the five seasons of *the wire* in his okcupid profile

no club in town has booked hayles after he changed his
name to "dj wolfbang amagayus throatzart"

minnie considers green day "oldies music"

andy moved to san francisco because it was more "laid-back"
and "anticonsumerist" than new york, but still manages to
drink two cups of starbucks a day

arthur keeps a moleskine notebook....it appears the entirety
of his pending novel is "buy batteries"

luna was so excited to be at sundance, she spent 80% of her time texting "i'm at sundance"

fozzie has that on blue vinyl

hamburglar paints antlers on everything

leila ruined the cupcake-decorating party after telling the story about how she hooked up with zach galifianakis

it only took five weeks for ross's darkroom to become ross's
grow room

dude, you haven't really chased your tail till you've done it on a fixed-gear bicycle

emma thinks the etsy store "would just love" her homemade, hand-stitched *lost in translation* puppets

hemingway claims *the watchmen* graphic novel is "one of the best pieces of literature of the 20th century," because he's read about five pieces of literature total

frankie's chillwave band vetoed his album art . . . even after he
went through all the trouble of drawing alf fucking a voltron

isabel is pondering whether it's a party foul to spin the *fresh prince of bel-air* theme

burt will have you know that he can taste the difference
between this and fair-trade coffee, thank you very much

linus finds the term "mailman" sexist, but still barks at him

cowboy called all cops "power-tripping nazi goons" until one found his stolen vespa

the summer after senior year, mr. cocomo traveled europe by train, and now aggravatingly insists that "it's bar*the*lona."

java doesn't want to tell vidna that she read only three pages before "nrrd grrl book club," so she plans to just nod and concur

vidna doesn't want to tell java that she only read three pages before "nrrd grrl book club," so she plans to just nod and concur

archibald is livid about the "evil new rite-aid" gentrifying his neighborhood, but totally psyched about the new apple store

gertrude was immoderately proud to be the only one knitting at the mastodon show

and with that, martin officially has more facebook photos
than facebook friends

teddy doesn't read pitchfork except when he reads pitchfork

ella bean bought the cutest old-timey banjo at an estate sale
two years ago, and it's been sitting in the hallway ever since

being neutered means the ability to wear even tighter jeans

theodore has convinced himself that spending $11 a day at the whole foods salad bar isn't exactly "eating out" since it's technically a grocery store

say anything is topper's favorite movie, favorite band and
most grating social tendency

tully wanted to bake you hash brownies but was so stoned
that she just made brownies

charlie insists that leaving snarky anonymous message
board comments is "part of his job"

ahahaha, look at this fucking asshole

zoey carries a record bag with her everywhere although it
has yet to hold an actual record

if this is as loud as these things go, wally honestly can't be in
a band with you

yuki dropped acid and thought, "what if it were the sticks that actually were fetching us?"

xino has completely sworn off high-fructose corn syrup—next stop, quitting cocaine!

billie cannot believe you put a tablespoon of butter in the
pasta when she's told you a thousand times that she's vegan

it's not a chew toy, it's a chew *collectible*

thanks for the gift, mom. . . . why exactly did you think i would like this?

THANK YOU

Danielle Perez and Paul Bresnick for putting up with me, Courtney Harris, Maura Johnston, Jennifer Daniel, Leah Greenblatt, Evie Nagy, Nick Chatfield-Taylor, BJ Warshaw, Jeanne Fury, Kory Grow, Jessica Suarez, Tom Mallon, Michelle Schwartz, Jen Ng, Heather Wagner and Alfred the pug, Al Shipley for inventing the word "pupster," kenan and Evan, Grayson Currin, Don Takano, Percy, Penny and Peanut

SPECIAL THANKS

This hilarious impulse buy is dedicated to whatever friend or relative gifts it as a last-minute birthday present. My electricity bill is paid with your procrastination and thoughtlessness.

Follow Hipster Puppies on Twitter: @hipsterpuppies.

Christopher R. Weingarten is a music critic living in Brooklyn whose work has been published in *The Village Voice*, *Spin*, RollingStone.com, *Revolver*, *Nylon*, *The Source*, *Decibel* and much more. His first book, a study of Public Enemy's *It Takes a Nation of Millions to Hold Us Back*, is out now from Continuum. His Twitter account is @1000TimesYes.

By official D&D rules, he is considered a "9th Level Hipster."